EXPLORE SHAPES AND ANGLES!

Jeanette Moore

Illustrated by Matt Aucoin

More titles in the **Explore Your World!** Series

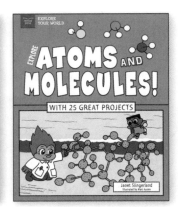

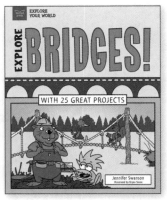

Check out more titles at www.nomadpress.net

Nomad Press
A division of Nomad Communications
10 9 8 7 6 5 4 3 2 1

This book was manufactured by Versa Press,
East Peoria, Illinois
October 2017, Job #J17-07607

ISBN Softcover: 978-1-61930-586-1
ISBN Hardcover: 978-1-61930-582-3

Educational Consultant, Marla Conn

Questions regarding the ordering of this book should be addressed to
Nomad Press
2456 Christian St.
White River Junction, VT 05001
www.nomadpress.net

Printed in the United States of America.

CONTENTS

Interested in primary sources? Look for this icon.
Use a smartphone or tablet app to scan the QR code and explore more!
You can find a list of URLs on the Resources page.

If the QR code doesn't work, try searching the Internet with the Keyword Prompts to find other helpful sources.

KEYWORD PROMPTS

shapes and angles

TIMELINE

3000–500 BCE:
Egyptians use geometry to measure amounts of crops. They also use math to build pyramids, tombs, and other structures.

1680–1620 BCE:
A scribe named Ahmes writes math documents about area and volume.

2000–500 BCE:
Ancient Babylonians make a list, since called Plimpton 322, that has geometric ideas on it about cubic measurement.

1500–200 BCE:
Indian mathematics is written in the ancient text of the Sulbasutras, including many measurement problems and methods for finding out the dimensions of circles.

1100–600 BCE:
Ancient Chinese mathematicians study right angles and triangles.

570–560 BCE:
Pythagoras of Samos travels the world to discover information about math and science. He is noted to be the "Father of the Right Triangle," though other people had discovered this before him.

400 BCE:
Euclid writes his famous book, *The Elements*, which is the foundation of the geometry we learn in school today.

350 BCE:
Hypatia is one of the first known female mathematicians. She studies geometry and translates classical mathematics books.

250 CE:
Liu Hui uses a polygon with 384 sides to figure out pi! He writes it in the book, *Nine Chapters*.

iv

1800–1900: Fractals are known as shapes found in clouds and fern plants. Once computers are invented, fractals are understood more.

1815–1852: Ada Lovelace works with Charles Babbage on patterns in math. She writes what is considered to be the world's first computer program.

1882–1935: Emmy Noether is called a mathematical genius by Albert Einstein. She creates the general foundation for Einstein's theory of relativity. She earns a PhD in math, but cannot get a job because she is female and Jewish.

1776–1831: Sophie Germain studies geometry and is the first woman to win a prize from the French Academy of Sciences.

1905: Albert Einstein creates the theory of relativity. There are many curves, spheres, and shapes in this theory.

1637: Rene Descartes writes *Discourse on the Method* and studies Euclid's dimensions.

2014: Maryam Mirzakhani becomes the first woman to be awarded the prestigious Fields Medal, awarded every four years to a young mathematition.

1963: Paul Cohen studies the continuum hypothesis, which states that numbers can go beyond infinity! This means they can go without limit.

GEOMETRY THROUGH HISTORY

Did you know you have been doing math since you were born? Geometry can be found everywhere in our world and we begin noticing it even as babies! Geometry was there in the bars of your crib, the round bowl of mushed peas you threw on the kitchen floor, and even within the space taken up by the liquid in your cup.

WORDS TO KNOW

geometry: the math related to shapes, surfaces, points, lines, and solids.

point: a spot in space or on a line.

lines: many points in a row that make one length.

length: the measure of something from one end to the other, or how long something is.

mathematics: the study of ideas related to numbers. Mathematicians study mathematics.

Geometry is a type of mathematics that we find all around us. In fact, geometry shows us the size of the earth and the size or amount of everything that's on the earth. Wherever you are right now as you read this, you are surrounded by geometry!

1

GE-OM-ET-RY

The word "geometry" has four syllables. Try saying it: Ge-om-et-ry. Let's take a look at all the parts of this word. *Ge* is an ancient Greek word meaning "Earth." The syllables "-metry" are an ending, or suffix. It shows that the word "geometry" has to do with a system. It comes from the ancient Greek word *metria*. That word is similar to the word "measure," which is one of the definitions of *metria*. When you measure something, you are figuring out how big something is, how much space it takes up, or how much it weighs.

Look across the room at an object. What do you see? How far away do you think it could be? Think about that object's shape. What is the size? These questions and thoughts are about geometry. You see—you are a mathematician, a person who studies math! Let's learn how geometry was part of our past.

GEOMETRY AND HISTORY

People started using geometry when our human ancestors went to work. They did not get in their cars and drive to the office or go to the store to take care of customers as your parents might do today.

Ancient humans had very different lives. They made tools for hunting. They made tools for cooking meals. Ancient humans built boats and homes.

2

Measuring and building were happening thousands and thousands of years ago. Our ancient relatives counted and tallied. They made scales and used weights. All this work was related to geometry!

This was true about their art, too. Art is full of curves and lines. Ancient people carved shapes, curves, and angles in caves, in rock, and on trees. And what about music? There are patterns in sounds as well, and in the wavelengths that each sound makes invisibly in the air. All this geometry was happening around the world, in the Americas, Australia, Asia, the Middle East, and Africa.

In 4200 BCE, ancient Egyptians created a solar calendar. To do this, they looked at the stars and made measurements and found patterns.

WHAT DID A BABY PYRAMID CRY OUT WHEN IT FELL?

I want my mummy!

The ancient Egyptians also did some large construction projects in the years after this calendar was made. This is when they built the ancient pyramids! That is some BIG geometry.

tally: to count the number of something.

scale: a tool used to weigh objects.

angle: the space between two lines that start from the same point, measured in degrees.

pattern: a series of repetitive connections and designs.

wavelength: the distance between two waves.

BCE: put after a date, BCE stands for Before Common Era and counts years down to zero. CE stands for Common Era and counts years up from zero. This book was published in 2017 CE.

solar calendar: a yearly calendar based on how long it takes the earth to move around the sun.

pyramid: a shape with a square base and triangles for sides that meet at a point.

square: a shape with four equal sides and four right angles.

triangle: a shape with three sides.

WORDS TO KNOW

Pyramids are enormous in size, but the invention of the wheel was just as important! In Mesopotamia, the wheel came about in 3500 BCE, but not for transportation. It was used as a potter's wheel to make round bowls and other containers. Eventually, wheels were stuck on a chariot to be ridden into battle!

The ancient Babylonians in Mesopotamia also worked with triangles called right triangles. They used rectangles and squares in their construction projects. These shapes all have right angles. Patterns, angles, and shapes were in their plans for cities.

In 2500 BCE, we can find geometry in India being used to plan big cities with streets and buildings. The Harrapan people, who lived in the Indus River Valley, made pottery with shapes and lines carved into the clay.

DID YOU KNOW?

The Babylonians were able to track Jupiter across the sky and make detailed records of the planets.

culture: a group of people and their beliefs and way of life.

circa (c.): around that year.

WORDS TO KNOW

Way across the Atlantic Ocean, in the region that is now Mexico and Central America, more people were using geometry. In about 1400 BCE, the ancient Olmec people made well-planned maps for cities and gardens. They also created a calendar.

In China in 550 BCE, scholars wrote a math book called the *Chou Pei Suan Ching*. This book discussed many geometry concepts, including right angles.

By 300 BCE, a mathematician named Euclid (c. 300 BCE) of Greece had finished a geometry textbook that we still consider useful today. Euclid came from Alexandria in Egypt. He studied math for many years and wrote his book, *The Elements*.

Geometry ideas came about in many cultures. They also spread from culture to culture as people moved around. Many cultures used geometry even before they officially called it geometry. They used shapes and angles to make plans for their cities, to build their homes, to measure time and the movements of planets, and to create art.

HYPATIA OF ALEXANDRIA

Hypatia of Alexandria (c. 350–415) was the first woman to teach geometry. She learned from her father, Theon of Alexandria, when they wrote about a new version of Euclid's book. Hypatia became head of the Platonist school at Alexandria, where she taught mathematics and science. She is the first woman in history recognized as a professional mathematician.

numerical value: a term to show numbers and their worth.

rhythm: a pattern of beats.

harmony: a pleasing blend of sounds.

WORDS ⊚ KNOW

PATTERNS IN OUR WORLD

We study geometry today for many of the same reasons the ancient civilizations did. In nature, there are numerical values all around us. Think about a garden of flowers. Each flower has a certain number of petals. Seeds in sunflowers follow a pattern. At the zoo, you might notice patterns in a tiger's stripes as well as on a turtle's hard shell.

Music has patterns, too. Think of your favorite beat and its sound, rhythm, and harmony. Each note creates a sound wave that follows a pattern.

In our neighborhoods, we use directions and move along with the help of maps. Builders construct homes and other buildings with different shapes. Angles and measurements are present in the objects we see, touch, and make.

There are shapes everywhere we look! There are also shapes that we cannot see. For example, the wireless networks we use for cell phones and the Internet have shapes and patterns. If you could see the wavelengths coming from a cell phone tower to one of these devices, they'd be circular!

SIGN LANGUAGE

Many patterns can be created with your fingers and hands. Did you know you can make shapes in order to communicate with others? This is called sign language. Try signing the letters for the word "love." The letter "L" is made by pointing your pointer finger straight up and your thumb straight out. The other three fingers are down. Now try the letter "O" by connecting your fingertips with the tip of your thumb to make an "O" shape. The next letter is "V," which looks just like a peace sign, or bunny ears! Then there is "E." Curl all of your fingers together inward and connect them with your thumb across the tips. L-O-V-E!

PS You can learn how to sign the alphabet with this video!

KEYWORD PROMPTS
ASL ABC Smart Hands

If geometry describes everything around us, does it describe us as well? Yes! You can find geometry not just with your body, but also on (and in!) your body.

In *Explore Shapes and Angles!*, we will take a field trip through our own bodies, our rooms, and outside to find the circles, squares, rectangles, triangles, and all different types of shapes, angles, and patterns. We'll discover what makes each shape and angle special and why some are stronger than others. We'll do lots of fun activities to find these shapes and use them in our own constructions. First, let's find geometry on our own bodies. Get ready to bend, twist, and move!

GOOD MATH PRACTICES

Every mathematician keeps a notebook with all of their calculations and observations. Choose a notebook to keep as your math journal. As you read through this book and do the activities, use a chart like the one below to help you keep track of your observations, data, and designs.

What I did:	Made different shapes by holding hands with people in different ways.
What I observed:	Our hands together made many different shapes.
What I learned:	Shapes and patterns are easy to find on our own bodies.
Questions I have:	Can I make more shapes with more people?

When doing an activity, remember that there is no right answer or right way to approach a project. Be creative and have fun!

Each chapter of this book begins with an essential question to help guide your exploration of shapes and angles. Keep the question in your mind as you read the chapter. At the end of each chapter, use your math journal to record your thoughts and answers.

? **INVESTIGATE!**

How many different shapes can you make with your hands and fingers?

PROJECT!

SHAKE HANDS ON IT!

SUPPLIES

✳ hands
✳ partners

You can make patterns by drawing and making objects. You can also make patterns with your own body! Find a partner and see what shapes you can make with your hands.

1 Shake hands with one person, two people, three people, then four people.

2 What do your palms and thumbs do when you shake hands with another person? Can you spot any shapes when your hands are together?

3 Stand face to face with a partner. Shake your right hand with their right hand. Hold on while you shake your left hand with their left hand. What letter did you make with your arms?

4 Try making handshake patterns with more than one partner. Everyone extend their right hands forward as if to give a regular handshake, but instead, have all the fingertips meet in the middle.

5 Then, everyone curl fingers at the same time, keeping the fingertips together. What do you notice?

TRY THIS! Make a group of five people. Everyone grab each other's wrists to create a shape in the center. What other shapes can you make? How many sides do your shapes have?

CHAPTER 1

MOVING, BENDING, STRETCHING GEOMETRY!

Head, shoulders, knees and toes, knees and toes,
Head, shoulders, knees and toes, knees and toes,
Head and shoulders, eyes and ears and nose,
Head, shoulders, knees and toes, knees and toes!

Remember that song from when you were little? You might not have realized this, but there is geometry in each of those body parts in the song. Your head, shoulders, knees, toes, eyes, ears, and nose all have geometry!

? INVESTIGATE!

What shapes and angles can you find on your body?

Your whole body is a great place to find lines, shapes, symmetry, and patterns. Let's take a look!

LEARN YOUR LINES!

An important lesson in geometry is how to find lines. A line is the shortest distance between points. A point is an exact location.

Stretch out your arm from shoulder to fingertip. You have made a line! Your shoulder and your fingertip are the points, and the arm between those points is a line.

symmetry: when a shape is the same when it is flipped, turned, or moved.

vertical: up and down.

horizontal: straight across from side to side.

parallel: lines that are side by side, with space between them.

intersect: lines that cross over or meet.

slope: the incline of a line.

equidistant: at equal distances.

WORDS ⌀ KNOW

There are different kinds of lines. Vertical lines travel up and down. Horizontal lines run across, left to right or right to left. Look around your classroom or home. Can you find vertical lines? Can you find horizontal lines? Can you find horizontal and vertical lines on your body?

Parallel lines run alongside each other. Parallel lines never intersect, or cross, one another. Parallel lines are like tracks in the snow left by a snowmobile. They run next to each other and the skis do not cross over one another. They must stay parallel to each other to get down a snowy slope. They are always the same distance apart, or equidistant.

On the other hand, perpendicular lines do cross one another! They intersect at a point. Where can you find perpendicular lines? Take a look at this lowercase "t." One line crosses over the other line.

That point of intersection makes the two lines perpendicular. Perpendicular lines can be found in letters, roads that have intersections and crosswalks, and even in cell phone towers. Can you spot any perpendicular lines on your own body? What happens if you make an X with your arms?

The lines you find make up shapes. A shape is the form that is made from lines that connect together. A shape can be a circle, a square, or a rectangle with four sides. What is the shape of a delicious slice of pizza? That most likely has a three-sided triangle shape. What about the shape of a house? This is a pentagon! A pentagon has five sides. We'll learn more about all of these shapes later in the book.

TOUCHDOWN!

Parallel lines are found in lots of sports! Take a look at a football field. The yard lines on a football field, including the 50-yard line, are parallel to one another and parallel to the field goal area. Can you find parallel lines on a soccer field? How about on a basketball court?

PUTTING THE ANGLE IN TRIANGLE

Let's take a closer look at triangles! There are three different types of triangles. A triangle can be equilateral, which is when all three sides are exactly the same length. In scalene triangles, each side is a different length. An isosceles triangle has two equal sides and one that is a different length.

equilateral: a type of triangle with three equal sides.

scalene: a type of triangle with three sides that do not equal one another.

isosceles: a type of triangle with two equal sides and one that is not equal.

hypotenuse: the side of a right triangle that is opposite the right angle. It is always the longest side of a right triangle.

WORDS ⊙ KNOW

Remember your slice of pizza? A slice is often the shape of an isosceles triangle, with the shorter side being the crunchy crust!

Stretch your arm out straight from your shoulder. Slowly bend your elbow up. Imagine a line connecting your shoulder to your fingertips to make a triangle. One of the sides of this triangle is made of your upper arm and another side is made of your lower arm.

Does the triangle stay the same as you raise your lower arm? What happens to the space above your elbow?

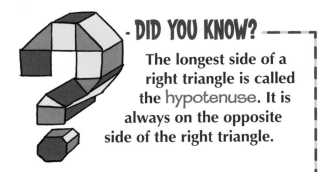

- DID YOU KNOW? --

The longest side of a right triangle is called the hypotenuse. It is always on the opposite side of the right triangle.

Triangles are made of angles. When two lines meet, they form an angle, unless they are meeting end to end to form a perfectly straight new line. When your upper arm is parallel to the floor and your lower arm is straight up and down, your elbow forms an angle that is 90 degrees, or a right angle.

If you move your hand closer to your shoulder, the angle becomes less than 90 degrees. This is called an acute angle. If you stretch your hand away from your shoulder and make the angle wider than 90 degrees, it becomes an obtuse angle. When you hold your arm out straight, your elbow is making a straight line, which has an angle of 180 degrees.

WHAT DO YOU CALL AN ADORABLE LITTLE ANGLE?

Acute angle!

14

quadrilateral: any shape with four sides.

WORDS ⊕ KNOW

Angles are everywhere! Can you find more angles on your body? What angles do your knees make? Can you make acute angles with your hands?

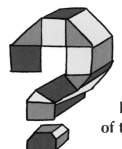

DID YOU KNOW?

Don't ever worry about math. Feeling confused because of math actually lights up the same areas of the brain as pain does!

A circle has 360 degrees. So does a rectangle! They are two different shapes with the same amount of degrees. How does that work?

Imagine two triangles. Each have a total of 180 degrees. If you place two right triangles together, with the two hypotenuses together, then you have a rectangle. The four angles of the rectangle will add up to 360 degrees. What if the two triangles are not right triangles? Your new shape will be a lopsided quadrilateral! No matter how lopsided it is, the new shape will have 360 degrees.

This is true for a perfect square. There are four angles in a square. Each of those angles is 90 degrees. If you add the four 90 degrees together, you will have 360 degrees!

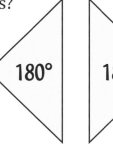
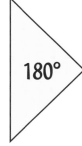

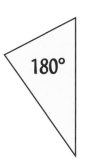

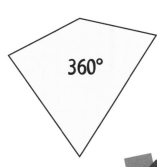

180° 180° 360°

180° 180° 360°

reflection: a mirror image.

line of symmetry: the imaginary line where you can fold a shape or picture and each half matches exactly.

WORDS ⊕ KNOW

THE FACE OF SYMMETRY

Take a look at your hand. Do you see parallel lines? Do you see perpendicular lines? Can you find vertical and horizontal lines? What happens to those lines if you tilt your hand sideways? Sometimes, the kind of line you see depends on how your hand is positioned!

Your two hands are very similar to one another. In fact, one looks like a reflection of the other. Look at your palms. Now place your pinky fingers next to each other. Fold your hands so one hand is against the other. Unfold the hands so the palms are face up again. That line where your pinkies meet creates a line of symmetry. A line of symmetry cuts a figure into two equal parts that mirror each other.

Can you find other parts of your body that are symmetrical? You can't fold your face in half, but if you could, it would be very close to symmetrical. How about your whole body?

SYMMETRY FACES!

Your face might seem symmetrical, but there are differences on each side. What would faces look like if they were truly symmetrical?

PS

You can see perfectly symmetrical faces at this website. They were created by an artist who took photographs and changed the picture so both sides are the same.

KEYWORD PROMPTS

Time perfectly symmetrical faces

HANDY PATTERNS

Patterns are made of shapes that repeat themselves. They are made of lines and shapes. We see patterns all the time. Are you wearing clothes with patterns?

If many people line up their hands and faces, we may find a pattern like this:

Two hands – One face – Two hands – One face

What happens if every person places one hand on either side of their face? Would that change the pattern? How about if everyone puts just one hand beside their face?

One face – One hand – One face – One hand

WHY SYMMETRY?

The human body is pretty symmetrical, but why? What use do we have for symmetry? Some scientists think that being symmetrical makes it easier for us to know how our bodies are positioned, so that we can balance better. Symmetry is also important for our eyes to sense distance and our ears to sense where a sound is coming from. Symmetry can be very useful!

What other patterns can you make with your hands and your face? Can you find patterns that are symmetrical? What patterns can you make with the angles you find on your body?

Some people say that math is the study of patterns. There are patterns everywhere when you're dealing with numbers! Skip counting is a form of pattern making. When we count by threes, we skip to each number that follows the first number in the sequence: 3, 6, 9, 12 . . . . That is a number pattern. The sequence 4, 8, 12, 16 is also a number pattern. What other types of skip counting can you do? What number patterns can you make?

Our bodies are where our understanding of geometry starts. Try the following activities and test your mathematician skills!

CONSIDER AND DISCUSS

It's time to consider and discuss: What shapes and angles can you find on your body?

HANDS DOWN GEOMETRY!

SUPPLIES

✳ newspaper
✳ orange ink pad, tempera paint, or fingerpaint
✳ white paper
✳ red pencil or crayon

Lines go in many different directions. Some lines never intersect. Other lines do. Some lines make small crisscross lines, such as the letter "x." Take a look at your own palms. What kinds of lines do you have in your palms?

1 Cover your work surface with newspaper. Place one hand gently in wet paint or on an ink pad. Do not soak your hand too much!

2 Put your hand onto the white sheet of paper. Press down hard.

3 Let your handprint dry, then trace the lines you see on it with a red pencil or crayon.

4 Find parallel, intersecting, and perpendicular lines. Every handprint is different!

5 Can you find an obtuse angle? An acute angle? A right angle?

6 Can you find shapes in the lines on your handprint? Look for triangles. What else can you find on your hand?

TRY THIS! Where else can you find lines on your body? Take off your socks! There are more parallel and perpendicular lines on the bottoms of your feet. Make footprints with your ink and see what lines, patterns, and shapes you can find.

PROJECT!

IN YOUR FACE!

Symmetry shows likeness. In addition to your hands, what other parts of the body are in pairs? Most people have two arms, two legs, and two feet, each with five toes. Let's take a closer look.

1 Prop the mirror up so you can see your face.

2 With your pencils, draw your face in your math journal.

3 Look at the symmetry in your face. You have two eyes. You have two nostrils. You have two eyebrows. What else do you have two of?

4 Now, look a bit deeper. For instance, look at one of the eyes you drew on the paper. Draw a straight line lightly through the eye, dividing it into two pieces. Is each side symmetrical?

5 Go back to other parts of your drawing and draw straight lines through small details. Check to see if the two sides are symmetrical or not. You can make your drawing more accurate this way!

THINK MORE: To take symmetry to the next level, use an easel or tape paper to the wall. Look at your whole body in the mirror. Draw your body so you can identify all the areas of symmetry. One half of your body is very similar to the other half. Color each set of symmetrical limbs different colors or create different designs on the paper to match them. Be creative!

PROJECT!

DOWNWARD FACING DOG

SUPPLIES

* ✳ yourself
* ✳ mirror, paper and pencil, camera

Downward Dog is a yoga pose created in ancient India that has been used for centuries. It's a terrific way to stretch your whole body! It's also a shape. Give this pose a try!

1 Start on your hands and knees. Place your wrists right under your shoulders and your knees right under your hips.

2 Spread your fingers wide. Stretch your arms out straight. Lift your knees off the floor and try to straighten your legs as you reach your bottom up to the ceiling. Your body will be in the shape of an upside-down "V", or a triangle.

3 Ask an adult to take a photo of you or look in a mirror. You can also have a partner draw a picture of you.

4 Are there any 90-degree angles? Can you spot any acute angles in your body? Can you find an obtuse angle?

TRY THIS! The world of yoga is endless. Try some more poses! Stand up straight with your hands and arms firmly by your sides. Now, stretch your two arms upward and reach for the sky. Let your arms begin to float downward but stop so that your body is making an uppercase "Y" shape. Lift your right leg off of the ground and bend it at the knee. Now, turn your leg so that your right foot is resting on the inside of your left thigh. You are now in tree pose. Can you balance? What are the shapes and angles created by your tree pose? Go ahead and try the other side!

PROJECT!

MAKING SHAPES WITH FRIENDS

Shaking hands with friends is easy, but can you make shapes with friends? Clear off a spot on the floor and give it a try!

1 Lay on the floor on your back. Keep your body straight.

2 Have a friend lay next to you about 3 or 4 feet away. Make sure the person is parallel to you.

3 Ask another person to lay down on the floor. This time, the person is perpendicular to you and your parallel buddy. This third person should have their feet by your head and their head by the parallel buddy's head.

4 Ask a fourth person to lay similarly to the third person, but by your feet instead of your head.

5 You have made a square with four people!

TRY THIS! What other shapes can you make? Try to make a triangle, pentagon, and hexagon.

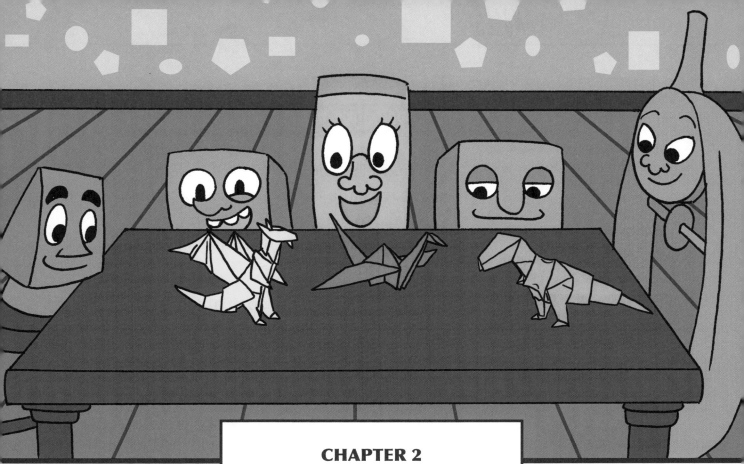

CHAPTER 2

ANGLES IN THE CLASSROOM

Shapes are everywhere! Look around your classroom. How many shapes can you see on your desk? How many can you see at the smartboard or chalkboard? Are there shapes on the walls and ceiling? What are some of the shapes you see?

You might find it easy to spot circles, squares, rectangles, and triangles. And you're sure to find parallel lines, perpendicular lines, and angles. Are there any other shapes in your classroom that you don't know the names for yet?

 INVESTIGATE!

Are there more polygons or polyhedrons in your classroom?

polygon: a shape with three or more straight sides and angles.

three-dimensional (3-D): something that appears solid and can be measured in three directions.

polyhedron: a 3-D shape.

line segment: two connected points that create a line.

WORDS TO **KNOW**

POLYGONS PRETTY MUCH EVERYWHERE

Your classroom is a good place to find shapes and patterns. It's also a good place to learn about polygons and three-dimensional (3-D) shapes called polyhedrons!

Any shape made up of at least three line segments, or line pieces, is called a polygon. The word *poly* means "many" in the ancient Greek language. When a shape is made of many lines, it is called a polygon!

There are a couple of rules for polygons. First, they have to have at least three lines. Second, all the lines need to connect. Third, none of the lines can be curved. Think about the triangles we discussed in the last chapter. Are they polygons? Do they follow the three rules? How about squares and rectangles?

Type of Polygon	Number of Sides		Type of Polygon	Number of Sides	
Triangle	3		Heptagon	7	
Quadrilateral	4		Octagon	8	
Pentagon	5		Nonagon	9	
Hexagon	6		Decagon	10	

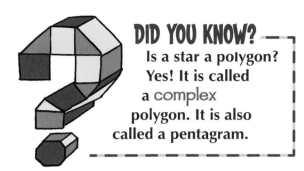

DID YOU KNOW?

Is a star a polygon? Yes! It is called a complex polygon. It is also called a pentagram.

Check out the chart to see the many kinds of polygons. You might have heard of a few of them already!

Look at the chart as a shape. How many sides does it have? What kind of polygon is it? A rectangle is a quadrilateral because it has four sides. Try to find other examples of quadrilaterals in your classroom.

Squares and rectangles are both examples of quadrilaterals. Another example of a quadrilateral is a shape called a rhombus. A rhombus is in the shape of a kite. It also looks similar to a diamond shape. A trapezoid is another kind of quadrilateral.

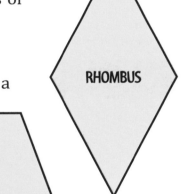

RHOMBUS

TRAPEZOID

FIND THE WORD CLUES

A tricycle has three wheels. A triangle has three sides. A triceratops has three horns. What do you think the word "tri" means? Three! You can find clues about what a word means from the parts of the word. *Quad* means "four" and *pent* means "five." What are some other clues you can find in the words for different polygons?

parallelogram: a four-sided shape with opposite parallel sides.

vertices: the corners where the lines of a polygon meet.

two-dimensional (2-D): something that appears flat and can only be measured in two directions.

width: the measure of something from one end to the other, or how wide something is.

depth: how deep something is, the measurement that gives a shape 3-D qualities.

height: the measure of how tall an object is.

WORDS ⊙ KNOW

Squares, rectangles, and rhombuses are all examples of quadrilaterals and parallelograms. They are quadrilaterals because they are shapes with four sides. They are parallelograms because their opposite sides are parallel.

All of these shapes have four sides. The line segments connect at the vertices, or corners, to make the shape. The four-sided shapes are in many objects you see every day.

POLYGONS IN 3-D!

We know paper as flat rectangles or squares. A piece of paper looks like a polygon! You can cut it into all sorts of shapes and sizes. But paper is flat. It is two-dimensional, or 2-D. In fact, all 2-D objects are flat. They are good to draw and cut, though! Circles, triangles, and pentagons are all 2-D. These are shapes that are made with lines and have length and width. But they do not have depth or height—they're flat.

The ancient Japanese art of folding paper into shapes is called origami. Origami is the process of folding paper to make a 3-D shape out of a 2-D shape. Origami uses just one square of paper for each finished shape. That one sheet of paper can be folded into thousands of different objects. Many geometric shapes emerge when the paper is folded over and over again. A blue piece of paper can turn into a beautiful crane or a sturdy boat. Shapes that are 3-D are called polyhedrons.

WHY ARE PAPER FOLDERS DANGEROUS?

They have a black belt in origami!

If a shape has depth, it is 3-D. You can draw 3-D shapes if you add extra lines to make the shapes look like something you can hold in your hand. The extra lines make the shapes have depth.

DID YOU KNOW?

A regular piece of paper cannot be folded more than seven times! The thickness of each fold requires lots of energy for the next fold. When it is folded seven times, it becomes very hard and crumbles!

Shapes that are 3-D almost look like they could pop off the paper! These are also good shapes for making models of out of playdough, cut paper, or cardboard.

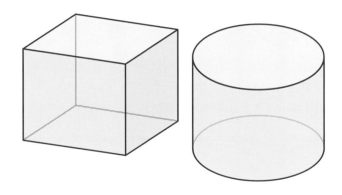

A polyhedron that might be familiar to you is found in freezers—ice cubes! A cube has six faces. Each face has four sides, like a square. A cube has 12 edges along those sides, where the faces meet. It also has eight vertices, or corners.

A polyhedron that has fewer faces, sides, and vertices than a cube is the tetrahedron. Each tetrahedron has four faces shaped like triangles, with three sides each. This shape also has four vertices and six edges. You can see a tetrahedron on the next page.

Your desk is a large, flat rectangle. But look at the side of the tabletop. It isn't actually flat like a piece of paper, is it? The tabletop has depth. While the top of the table's flat surface may be 2-D, the tabletop itself is 3-D.

DID YOU KNOW?

A tetrahedron is a 3-D shape made of four 2-D triangles.

GREAT PYRAMIDS!

Pyramids have a square base and four sides that look like triangles. Ancient Egyptians are well known for building pyramids. Pyramids were also built in Peru and other areas of the world. In Egypt, the pyramids were used as tombs! The leader, known as a pharaoh, was buried in the pyramid when he died. More than 130 pyramids have been found in Egypt. A boy king was discovered in one of them. King Tutankhamun was a pharaoh when he was only nine years old!

prism: a solid shape whose two end faces are similar, equal, and parallel and whose sides are parallelograms.

WORDS ⊙ KNOW

If the whole tabletop is 3-D, it isn't really a rectangle. Yes, the surface is a rectangle. But the whole top is a rectangular prism. This is the name for a 3-D rectangle. The "prism" part adds depth to the object.

Type of Polyhedron	Number of Vertices	Number of Edges	Number of Faces	
Tetrahedron	4	6	4	
Cube	8	12	6	
Octahedron	6	12	8	
Dodecahedron	20	30	12	

What is a 3-D triangle called? That is a triangular prism! Think of a slice of pizza. The thick crust and layers of sauce and toppings give the triangle depth, turning it into a 3-D shape. That's a 3-D snack!

TRANSFORMERS!

No matter what shape an object is, it can always transform. A transformation is the way a shape can move along a grid or graph. These movements include translation, which is when a shape slides over to the left or right. There is also reflection, which is when a shape has a mirror image. Dilation is when shapes get larger or smaller. Have you noticed that your pupil, the black center of your eye, gets larger when the lights are dim? That's dilation!

Lastly, shapes can rotate. Rotation is when shapes move around in a circle. These turns make it move around, like a carousel or ferris wheel.

Look around your classroom. From paper to desks to chairs to smartboards and blackboards, geometry can be found in your classroom! What other shapes and patterns can you find around your desk?

? **CONSIDER AND DISCUSS**

It's time to consider and discuss: Are there more polygons or polyhedrons in your classroom?

PROJECT!
POLYGON PILE-UP

SUPPLIES

* ✳ paper
* ✳ pencil
* ✳ objects around the classroom
* ✳ ruler or stencil
* ✳ scissor
* ✳ glue or tape

Polygons are found in the classroom, but we can cut polygons out of paper, too. Polygons might seem like basic circles, rectangles, and squares, but the more sides you add, the more complex the polygons become! What if you join two or more polygons together to make a new shape or a design? Take a look below!

1 Take a piece of paper and trace a shape. Look at the chart on page 24. Pick a polygon! Or two! Or five!

2 You can also use an object in your classroom to trace shapes. For example, use a rectangular eraser to trace a small rectangle. What can you use to make a circle? A triangle? Use scissors to cut the traced or drawn shapes.

3 Take all of the polygons and make a design. Or a robot! Many things are made up of many different shapes. What can you create from your polygons?

4 Tape or glue your shapes together. Fold your design. Is there symmetry? If not, you can add more shapes to make the design symmetrical.

TRY THIS! You can create everyday items with the polygons you cut. But can you create an invention? Design something with your shapes that has never been made before. Give your invention a name and write about what it can do. Present it to the class!

PROJECT!

3-D SHAPESHIFTERS!

SUPPLIES

* feet, legs, hands and arms
* partner (or 2 or 3!)

You don't have to find dice to see what a cube looks like. You don't have to hunt for a tetrahedron either. You can make these 3-D shapes with a few friends, using arms and legs. And suddenly you unite and become shapeshifters!

1 First, make a two-person cube. With a partner, sit on the floor. Face one another. Place your legs out in front, straight on the floor. Now, spread your legs like a "V."

2 Connect your feet with your partner's feet. You made a square! That is just one face of the cube though.

3 Next, open your arms. They are parallel to your legs. Touch your fingertips to your partner's fingertips. A two-person cube!

4 Ask two more friends to join in. One sits where you and your partners' feet meet on one side, and the other sits where you and your partner's feet meet on the other side. They can extend their legs in a "V" shape as well. Their arms will open too. Their fingertips meet yours and then your partner's fingertips. A four-person cube!

5 With two people, you can make a tetrahedron. Each person raises their right arm. Lean in and touch fingertips. It almost looks like a tent.

6 Stretch your left arm into the armpit of the person next you. Don't tickle them! You've made a tetrahedron with four triangular faces.

TRY THIS! If you have four people or more, there are many shapes that can be made. One person can act as the photographer and take a picture of the shapes your group is making. Another person can be the director who guides you to make an interesting shape or pattern. You can plan to make a letter. You may even want to spell a word! Think of the letter "M." Consider how many legs it has: four. Two people can lay down, making parallel lines for the left and right sides of the "M." Then two more people can form a "V" in the center of the two parallel lines to complete the "M." What words can you spell?

PROJECT!

STOP, DROP, AND FOLD!

SUPPLIES

✳ sheets of paper

Shapes make up everyday objects. We can cut shapes from paper, but also make new shapes through folding. Let's focus on rectangles. With some flips and folds, we will have something to place on our heads!

1 Fold your rectangular piece of paper in half, the long way. Open it up.

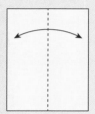

2 Fold the top down to the bottom edge. Fold the top corners down to the line that runs down the center.

3 Fold the bottom edge of the top layer up to the base of the triangles. Fold this part up again.

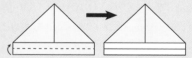 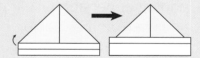

4 Turn the paper over. Do step 3 again. Open the hat to shape it. You are done!

34

PROJECT!

TRY THIS! A hat takes only a few steps to complete. How about a frog?

1 Fold a piece of paper in half, the long way. Open it up.

2 Fold both top corners to the opposite edges of the paper. See where the diagonal creases meet in the middle? Fold the paper backward and then open it.

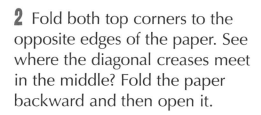
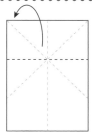

3 Hold the paper at the sides of that fold. Bring the points down to the center line. Flatten the paper.

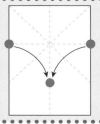

4 Fold the top triangles up to the tippy top point. Fold the sides to the line in the center.

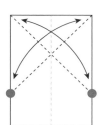

5 Fold the bottom of the model up so the bottom edge sits on the center of the top diamond (a rhombus!). Fold the same part down and in half.

6 Turn over the frog! Draw on some eyes. To make it jump, press on the lower back.

35

PROJECT!
CUBE ART

Cubes aren't just for plopping into a cup of juice or water to make it cold! Cubes are also fun to draw on. How? Find out below.

1 Go to this website to print the cube template and cut it out of the paper. http://babbledabbledo.com/wp-content /uploads/2015/02/Doodle-Cube-Template-.pdf

KEYWORD PROMPTS

doodle cube template

2 Decorate the cube with shapes and lines. Try to do continuous designs. Those are ones you can see on more than one face of the cube.

3 Cut out the cube. Fold it along the lines shown in the template. Tape or glue the sides together along the edges.

4 Make several cubes and create a portrait of someone you know. Your final artwork might not look exactly like the person, but does it represent certain parts of their personality?

TRY THIS! Team up with classmates who have cubes. Build an object or a tower with many cubes. What colors and designs do you all have in common? What is different? Get ideas from seeing others' cubes. You might add to your cube, or design it further. You can use other arts and crafts, such as glitter glue, stickers, and sequins.

CUBISM

Cubism is a type of art that was popular more than 100 years ago. Artists sketched and painted many shapes and cubes in their pictures. This type of art was abstract and modern. It was new and many people didn't like it! Pablo Picasso and Paul Cézanne were two artists who introduced shapes and cubes into their art. From then on, the art world changed shape!

PS **You can see paintings in the cubism style at this website.**

KEYWORD PROMPTS

Tate cubism 🔍

PROJECT!
POETRY PATTERNS

Sentences, words, and letters all follow patterns. This is especially true for rhymes and syllables. Poems have patterns based on their words and the way they are written. What if you made a poem about a shape, and then the paper was in the shape of the shape that you wrote about? That almost sounds like a tongue-twister!

SUPPLIES

* square- or rectangular-shaped paper
* scissors
* pencils, markers, or crayons

1 Decide on a polygon shape you want your poem to be in. Cut your paper into that shape.

2 On a piece of scratch paper, work on a poem about the shape that you chose. You can try to make your poem rhyme or simply write a free verse, which is a poem that doesn't rhyme.

Diamond
Pointy, four-sided
Sparkling, digging, wishing
Ring, star, window, clown eyes
Winking, spinning, waiting
Transparent, sharp
Diamond

3 When you are happy with your poem, write your final draft on your shape. Your poem will reflect the shape of the paper it's written on!

TRY THIS! Try the poetry writing on a polygon, but then fold your polygon-shaped poem into an origami shape! Use the hat or frog origami instructions on pages 34 and 35, or research a new animal or object to fold.

38

EXPLORING AND TRANSFORMING

SUPPLIES

* objects in the classroom, such as a ruler, piece of paper, book, lunchbox, crayon box, and more
* pencil
* math journal

Get ready to explore! You do not need a magnifying glass or even a telescope. You will be exploring your classroom. There is plenty to discover!

1 Gather objects in the classroom or from your desk or backpack. Line up your objects on your desk.

2 In your math journal, make a chart like the one below.

Draw the object	Rotate one quarter	Rotate one half	Rotate three quarters	Rotate all the way (full circle)

3 Draw an object in the left box. Then, rotate it one-quarter of the way around. That is like when the clock has the second hand on the 15 (one quarter past the hour). Draw what the object looks like.

4 Continue with the rotations and draw what each object looks like. What happens with each shape when it is turned one quarter? One half? Three quarters?

TRY THIS! Draw each object and then draw its reflection. Draw an object that has symmetry. For example, draw a butterfly. Now fold the paper in half. Is one half the reflection of the other half? Improve the drawing so it is an exact reflection.

CHAPTER 3

MEASURING YOUR HOME AND YARD

• • • • • • • • • • •

After a long day at school, you arrive home and toss your backpack by your desk. Your brain needs a break! Whether you head outside or stay in for some quiet time, it's always a great idea to recharge at the end of a school day.

• •

Even as your brain is focused on playing games or eating snacks, you can still spot geometry all around you! Lines, shapes, and angles are everywhere in your house. They are inside and outside your home.

? INVESTIGATE!

What might your house look like if the builder hadn't measured anything? Why is it important to measure the sizes of things?

You can find geometry on the roof, in the elevator, and in the staircases! Geometry is all over the backyard, the patio, and the porch. It is in flowers, tree rings, and leaves. Take a stroll outside and look around—what do you see?

HOW BIG IS BIG?

Look around your living room or bedroom. What is the biggest book in the room? What is the tallest piece of furniture? What is the heaviest object? To measure how big or long or tall or heavy something is, we use tools of measurement.

One tool of measurement is the ruler. The units of measure on a ruler can be standard measurement or metric. Standard measurement is used only in the United States, Burma, and Liberia. Metric measurement is used everywhere else!

TREEHOUSE LIVING

Today, some people live in treehouses that have running water, kitchens, and even toilets! Fifty years ago in the South Pacific, a tribe was discovered in New Guinea that had lived in the canopy of the forest trees for decades. This tribe is called Korowai. What kinds of shapes do you think they see from up there?

dimension: any line of a shape that can be measured.

WORDS ⊙ KNOW

Metric measurement is based on the number 10. Standard measurement is based on objects people were familiar with in past cultures.

When you are measuring something small, a ruler is a useful tool. Many rulers measure in inches (standard measurement) and centimeters (metric measurement). These units of measurement give the length of an object.

DID YOU KNOW? ─────────

Length, width, and height or depth are different dimensions of a shape. Length and width measure two different dimensions on a flat surface. Height or depth measure how high something is or how deep it is, giving an object three dimensions.

Everything you see can be measured! Imagine walking through a door. What shape is the door? What is the height of the door? How wide is the door? The study of geometry includes learning how to measure different shapes!

The doorway is a space you must walk through to get outside. Even that rectangular space has dimensions. Dimensions are another word for measurements. A dimension is how tall something is, or its height. Dimensions also include the length and width, or how long and wide something is.

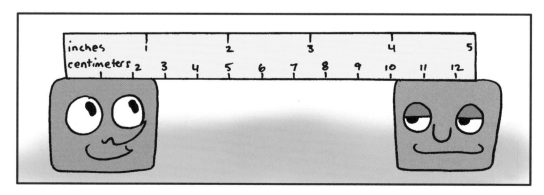

layout: the way the parts of something are arranged.

WORDS TO KNOW

How tall is the door or the doorway? If you don't have a measuring tape and you know how tall you are or how long your arms are, you can use your body to measure. Reach your arms out perpendicular to the floor or stretch your arm up high. Arms can serve as good tools to make estimates for dimensions.

Estimates are good guesses. When you estimate the length of something, you compare the length of something you know with what you want to measure. This way, you can get a good idea of what the measurement is without using any other tool.

You can check to see if your estimate is correct by using a tool. Carpenters and builders use tape measures. This tool is like a long ruler that rolls up and fits into a small holder. It can be placed on a belt or in a toolbox. Have you ever used a tape measure?

INSIDER DESIGN

Interior designers are people who design rooms to make them look a certain way and feel inviting. They decide what colors to paint the walls, what fabrics will be used in the curtains, and where the furniture will go. To make the spaces feel comfortable, they work to understand the layout of the house. It is important for interior designers to have the measurements of all the rooms and what will go in them so everything can fit! Designers also use geometry to figure out what patterns are best for wallpaper, blankets, and pillows. Designers consider shapes, colors, and different textures to make a room look and feel a certain way.

weight: the measure of the force of gravity on an object.

gravity: a force that pulls objects toward each other, and all objects to the earth.

WORDS TO KNOW

Once you've done your estimating and measuring of the door, you can walk through and find more things to measure out on your porch and in the yard. Is there a set of chairs? Is there a table? What are the shapes you see?

HEAVY LIFTING!

Another thing to measure is the weight of an object. Look around outside for something that has weight. Find a tiny rock. Can you feel its weight in your hand? Find a larger item, such as a baseball bat or a small shovel. Is this heavier?

We can measure weight with a measurement tool called a scale. In standard measurement, we measure in pounds. If you place a book on a scale, it can be weighed in pounds. In the metric system, the book is measured in kilograms. These two units of measurement come in handy when we weigh objects.

PS

Gravity is different on other planets, so your weight would be different, too. **Check out what your weight would be around the solar system at this website!**

KEYWORD PROMPTS

Exploratorium weight

WEIGHING WITH ROCKS

For decades, the scale has been a tool used for measurement. What was used before the modern scale? How did people weigh objects? One of the earliest known scales used a rod and two pans. A rod had some kind of string attached on each end. A pan was attached to each string. The object to be weighed was placed in one pan. Rocks with known weights were placed in the other pan until the two sides balanced. This is how people used to weigh things!

Measuring the dimensions of space and shapes is an important skill to have. Knowing an object's measurements means you can compare that object to others to find out more information. Let's take a look how!

MORE TYPES OF MEASURING

Say you are eating a slice of pizza at the picnic table in your backyard. Then, a friend comes to visit. You offer them a slice of pizza. You can eat together!

The two of you compare your pizza slices. What are the chances that the slices have the exact same measurements?

DID YOU KNOW? —
Weight is caused by gravity. Gravity is what pulls us and all objects toward the earth. This pull is what gives us a weight. How much do you weigh?

congruent: when two shapes are the same as each other.

WORDS ⊕ KNOW

Not likely! Pizza slices might look similar, but when you measure them, you find they are slightly different. If they were exactly the same, with the same lengths of the sides and the same triangular shape, then the two slices of pizza would be called congruent.

You might have congruent slices if the pizza came from the same restaurant. You might have congruent slices if the slices were cut in the same way. Most of the time, though, even when the pizza comes in the same box and is part of the same pie, each slice is a little different.

What about the picnic table? Are there any parts of the table that are congruent? The tabletop has two lengths, the length along the top and the length along the bottom. These two lengths are congruent. The two widths are also congruent. Can you find other objects in your yard that are congruent?

When building something, such as a pool or a building, it is important to have equivalent, or equal, measurements. This means the height on one side of the deep end of the pool must be equivalent to the height on the other side of the deep end of the pool. That way, the pool won't be lopsided!

WHO IS KING OF THE PENCIL CASE?

A ruler

Equivalent parts are especially important when building a home. The floors must have equivalent-sized wooden boards. The beams that hold the home up must be equivalent. The walls must be equivalent, too, or else you'll have to duck in certain corners! The roof must have equivalent sides as well. What would happen to a building that was not constructed with equivalent pieces of wood and steel?

RECYCLING STEEL

Almost 69 percent of all steel in North America is recycled every year. Steel has magnetic properties that make it the easiest material to separate from other waste. Every year, recycling steel saves enough energy to power almost 18 million households. Steel is found in everyday products we use. For example, steel latches on car doors help keep the doors latched during an accident. And the safety buckles for seat belts are made with steel!

"Congruent" and "equivalent" are geometry terms that often get confused. Think of it like this: We use the word congruent when we talk about the shape of an object. If two shapes can be placed exactly over one another without any extra sticking out, they are congruent. You can flip them or rotate them to see. If the measurements of two shapes are exactly the same, those shapes are equivalent.

Can you find congruent shapes in your backyard? Can you find equivalent shapes?

Learning to measure is an important part of learning geometry! Take your measuring skills beyond your backyard and discover the dimensions of more things in your neighborhood.

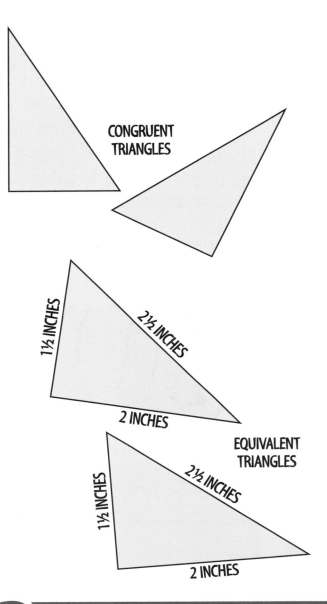

CONGRUENT TRIANGLES

EQUIVALENT TRIANGLES

1½ INCHES
2½ INCHES
2 INCHES

1½ INCHES
2½ INCHES
2 INCHES

? CONSIDER AND DISCUSS

It's time to consider and discuss: What might your house look like if the builder hadn't measured anything? Why is it important to measure the sizes of things?

PROJECT!

DREAM TREEHOUSE

Do you ever dream? Many kids have dreams in the night or they look out of the window and have a "daydream." You can use your imagination to get creative and dream up a dreamy treehouse!

SUPPLIES

* ✳ pencil
* ✳ graph paper with boxes ½ inch by ½ inch or smaller— you can find graph paper online to print

KEYWORD PROMPTS

print graph paper 🔍

1 On your graph paper, draw a big tree with a large amount of space in the leafy branch area.

2 Within the branches, draw one or two rooms that are as big or as small as you want. Use the squares on your graph paper to guide you. For example, one room in your tree house may be seven squares long and five squares wide. Label the length and width of the sides.

3 Color and design your house! What is in that room? Is it filled with cozy pillows and fluffy blankets? That would be a comfy treehouse room!

TRY THIS! Perhaps your treehouse needs a bit of wallpaper. Wallpaper often has a repeated pattern. Use a new piece of graph paper to create a pattern. Maybe you could color half of every square or alternate colors with each square. Repeat the pattern throughout the entire piece of graph paper to see what it might look like on a wall.

SWINGY BIRD FEEDER

Making dream treehouses is fun, but what lives in the trees? Birds! Hang this feeder from a branch or near a tree. Watch birds flock to their dream feeder!

1 Lay out the popsicle sticks side by side to make the bottom of the feeder. It should take about 11 sticks. Make sure it is a square by using one stick as a measuring tool to check the length. Each stick must be parallel and congruent.

2 Add glue to two more sticks. Place them across the base at each end. This will secure the bottom of the feeder! Add two more sticks across the middle to make the base more stable. These four sticks are perpendicular to the base sticks.

3 When the glue dries, flip the base over. Add two sticks along the top and bottom of the base. The two sticks should be perpendicular to the base sticks.

4 Add glue to the corners of these two sticks. Add sticks to overlap these sticks, like you are building a small log cabin. Repeat this about 20 times. Let your bird feeder dry.

5 Cut two pieces of string. Each string should be 1 foot long. Use your ruler! One foot is 12 inches.

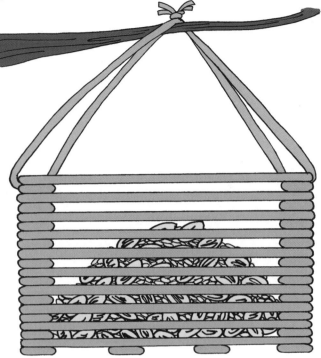

6 Weave one of the strings down through the slats on the left side and then back up. Do the same for the right side. Tie the four ends together in one large knot.

7 Fill your feeder with birdseed and find a nice place to hang the feeder for the birds.

TRY THIS! What kinds of birds visit your bird feeder? Write down the characteristics of the birds you see. You can find out about different birds by looking at this website.

KEYWORD PROMPTS

all about birds 🔍 ←

PROJECT!

BUBBLY PRISM

SUPPLIES

* ½ cup dish detergent
* 4 tablespoons glycerin
* 4½ cups water
* bowl and spoon
* clay
* scissors
* drinking straws
* toothpicks

Bubbles do more than fizz in seltzer or pop when you step on bubble wrap. Bubbles might be filled with air, but they take shape, too. Bubbles can be made with soap. Get ready to get squeaky clean!

1 Make some bubble solution by mixing the dish detergent, glycerin, and water in a bowl.

2 Build a prism! Shape eight small balls of clay. Cut the straws into 12 pieces that are all the same length as a toothpick. Make sure they are all as congruent as possible!

3 Place a toothpick inside one straw piece. Put a small ball of clay on one end. Repeat this process until you have four toothpick straws that you can connect to make a square. Make another square the same way.

4 Connect these two squares with four more of your toothpick straws. You will have a cube!

5 Plop the prism gently into the bowl of bubble solution. Pick it up slowly. What happens? Try dipping it again. Do you get a different bubble shape?

TRY THIS! Make different polyhedrons out of toothpicks, straws, and clay and try them in the bubble solution. What happens to the shape of the bubble when the shape of the frame changes?

PROJECT!

GEOMETRIC GARDEN

The plots of land where farmers and gardeners grow crops is often a familiar 2-D shape, such as a square or a rectangle. What other shapes can you find in a garden?

SUPPLIES

* small plot of land or rectangular pot
* small shovel
* tape measure
* soil
* flower seeds, such as morning glories
* pencil and paper

1 Measure a small sunny plot of land, 2 feet by 3 feet. If you want, you can use a rectangular pot to put on your porch or in your kitchen.

2 If you are in the yard, dig up the grass, remove rocks, and make sure the soil is good and loose for seeds! Surround the edges of the plot of land with rocks. If you have a rectangular pot, add soil to the pot and smooth it with your shovel.

3 Measure how far apart the seeds need to be planted. If the package says they need to be 4 inches apart and your plot is 3 feet long, or 36 inches, how many seeds will you plant? How far apart must each seed be?

4 Sketch a diagram of your garden plot in your math journal with your measurements. Using your diagram, plant your seeds. Don't forget to water them!

TRY THIS! What other shapes can you make your garden? There are circle-shaped gardens, U-shaped gardens, triangle-shaped gardens, and even heart-shaped gardens. Plan an "oddly" shaped garden. Put seeds in alternating patterns, by flower type or by color.

WORDS TO KNOW

crop: a plant grown for food and other uses.

PROJECT!
MINI SCALE MODELS

How big is your deck or your yard? It might be many feet long, but it can be shrunk down to a tiny little drawing. Let's see how!

SUPPLIES

* math journal
* measuring tape
* pencil
* graph paper

1 Measure the length and width of your yard or deck. Write these measurements in your math journal.

2 Measure objects in your yard or on your deck. Write down the length and width of each object.

3 Now, make a scale factor. For example, one foot can be equal to one square on your graph paper. So if your deck is 14 feet long, then the length of the drawing of your deck is 14 squares long!

4 Construct your mini deck or mini yard on your graph paper.

5 Add all the objects, such as chairs and picnic tables, into your drawing. Color your mini model of your deck or yard!

TRY THIS! Take the measuring tape inside! Measure different rooms and draw scale models of each. Guess what? You are making a **blueprint**, just like an **architect**!

54

WORDS TO KNOW

blueprint: a model or detailed plan to follow.

architect: a person who designs structures.

CHAPTER 4

SHIP-SHAPES IN THE NEIGHBORHOOD

Geometry extends way beyond our bodies, our classrooms, and our yards. Geometry is present in the community, too. It does not matter if you live in a busy city or a rural area. There is evidence of geometry all around you!

What do you see when you take a walk through your neighborhood? You might notice roads and sidewalks. There could be fences and walls. Do you have local restaurants and diners in your neighborhood? Are there many trees and fields?

? **INVESTIGATE!**

Why is it important to know the area, perimeter, or volume of a space or object?

Most buildings are rectangular prisms, which are 3-D shapes with a rectangle for a base. They are tall structures with six flat faces, just like a cube. It also has right angles like a cube. And it has eight points, or vertices, like a cube!

What is the difference between a cube and a rectangular prism? The length, width, and depth of a rectangular prism are not all equal the way they are in a cube.

Look for more polyhedrons in your neighborhood. Take a stroll to the playground. There are lots of shapes there! Perhaps the slide is a cylinder tube. A bridge is made of rectangular prisms. A half of a sphere might peek out from the top of the playset. A half of a sphere is called a hemisphere.

PERIMETER AND AREA

In the last chapter, we discussed measuring smaller items, such as tables and doorways. How do we measure large areas? How do we measure an entire park? For that, we need to use perimeter and area!

The perimeter of a shape is when the measurements of all the sides of a shape are added together. For example, let's say there is a table at your neighborhood park. The top of the table is a rectangle. The two short sides of the rectangle tabletop each measure 40 inches. And the two long sides of the rectangle tabletop each measure 60 inches. Add all the sides up!

40 inches + 40 inches + 60 inches + 60 inches = 200 inches

The perimeter of the table is 200 inches. The perimeter is the total number of inches measured around the shape and added together. This is the length of all the sides of the shape.

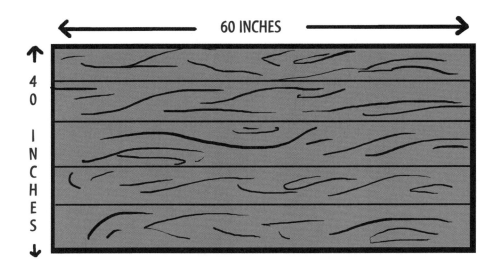

60 INCHES

40 INCHES

square inch: a unit of area that measures length times width, in inches.

WORDS ⊙ KNOW

The area of the table in the neighborhood park is a little different. To find the area of the tabletop, the length and width must be multiplied.

The length of the tabletop is 60 inches. This is the long part of the picnic table. The width of the table is 40 inches. This shows how wide the tabletop is. To find the area of the table, multiply the length and the width.

60 inches x 40 inches = 240 square inches

The area of the table is 240 square inches.

Square inches! Why not use regular inches? The rectangle's area shows how many square units can be contained in that shape, or how many 1-inch squares could fit onto the tabletop. If you were planning on painting the top of the table, you'd know that you needed 240 square inches of paint to have enough to cover the whole tabletop.

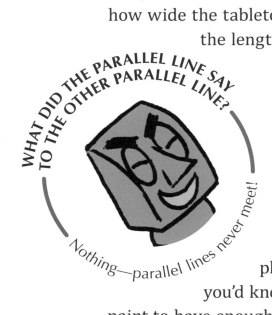

WHAT DID THE PARALLEL LINE SAY TO THE OTHER PARALLEL LINE?

Nothing—parallel lines never meet!

This method would work if you wanted to paint the outside of the houses and other buildings in your neighborhood. Measuring the outside can tell a painter how many cans of paint they need. It can tell a construction worker how many boards they need. Knowing the area will help a window installer get the right amount of glass for windows and doors in a building.

DID YOU KNOW?

The Kansas City Public Library in Missouri has a parking garage that looks like a book shelf! Each book on this pretend shelf is about 25 feet tall and 9 feet wide!

The pavers who pave the parking lots have to know how much tar is needed. The workers making sidewalks must know how much concrete they need. How wide are the sidewalks? How long are they? This is true for roads as well. And even highways! That is a *lot* of tar to measure for.

Perimeter and area are important things to know about indoor spaces, too. People need to know the area of a room if they want to buy carpet or put in wooden floors. They need to know the area of each wall so they can buy the right amount of wallpaper.

There are important questions that need to be asked and answered . . . even when just measuring that table at the park!

RIDE THE ROADS

The geometric designs of roads are handled by **engineers**. There are three main parts that make up road design. There is alignment, which is how the road will be made horizontally and what curves the road will have. There is also the profile. The profile is how high or low a road goes. Last, there is the cross section. This allows engineers to understand where the drains should be, how wide bike lanes need to be, and how many cars can go on the road. Roads must be constructed in a safe way for neighborhoods everywhere. Engineers help!

WORDS TO KNOW

engineer: someone who uses science, math, and creativity to design and build things.

volume: the amount of space inside a shape.

cubic feet: a unit of volume that measures length times width times depth (or height), in feet.

WORDS ⊚ **KNOW**

THE COMMUNITY POOL NEEDS WATER!

If there was a community pool at your local recreation center, the workers at the community pool would need to keep it filled with water. A truck might come and fill up the pool the first time. How do the workers know how much water should go in the pool? They need to find out the volume of the pool to know how much water to bring.

The pool has length, width, and depth (or height). Maybe it is 4 feet deep. The length of the sides are 10 feet each. The width is 9 feet on each of the shorter sides. To find the volume, multiply the length times the width times the depth.

4 feet x 10 feet x 9 feet = 360 cubic feet

DESIGN A SIDEWALK

Sidewalk design is a job for an engineer! It's important that engineers plan safe sidewalks for people who want to walk, bike ride, and do other activities on sidewalks. When a sidewalk is designed, engineers decide how long and wide it will be. They also consider the material they will use, such as concrete. And they want to be sure the sidewalks are not too steep, or else they will be hard to climb!

PS Watch a video of artists using sidewalks as a place to make art!

KEYWORD PROMPTS

3D sidewalk chalk art 🔍

HOW DO CONSTRUCTION WORKERS PARTY?

They raise the roof!

This is the volume of the pool! That is the total amount of water the pool can hold. And it is measured in cubic feet, which means feet cubed, because the length, width, and depth make it 3-D.

What happens on a really hot day when everyone in your town goes swimming at the pool? The water rises! What happens if too many people go into the pool at once? The water will overflow!

Your body has volume, too. Workers can never fill the community pool all the way to the tippy top and then have 50 people hop in, or there will be a big flood of water leaving the pool! When considering how much water to put in the pool, workers keep the volume of bodies in mind so that flood doesn't happen.

glacier: a slowly moving mass of ice and snow.

WORDS ⊙ KNOW

A community pool can hold a large volume of water, but the entire planet can hold even more. The volume of water on Earth is tremendous! The surface of Earth is about 71 percent covered in water. The oceans hold about 97 percent of that water. Water is also in the form of a gas in the air, in the form of liquid in rivers and lakes, and in the form of ice in glaciers. The water volume of all the oceans, seas, and bays on Earth is measured in cubic miles—321,000,000 cubic miles! There is also water in the soil. On Earth, the water volume of soil moisture is 3,959 cubic miles.

Now that you know how to spot examples of geometry in your neighborhood, let's venture farther afield and see what shapes and patterns we can find in nature!

CONSIDER AND DISCUSS

It's time to consider and discuss: Why is it important to know the area, perimeter, or volume of a space or object?

CIRCLE IT!

Circles are another shape you'll find in the neighborhood! Circles are special, because the distance between the center point and any point on the circle is the same—this is called the radius. If you drew a straight line from a point on the circle through the center point to a point on the other side of the circle, you'd be drawing the diameter. Circumference is the measure of the circle all the way around. And pi, or π, is the circumference divided by the diameter of the circle, which is always about 3.14, no matter how big or small the circle is!

RUB A DUB DUB . . . WALL?

SUPPLIES

* tracing paper
* crayons with the outer wrapping removed or colored chalk

Rubbings can be made of carvings that we may find in the community. There are markers along streets where important events have occurred. There are engravings in walls and benches and on plaques. What do you see on manhole covers? Get ready to make a rubbing!

1 Take a walk in your community. Pay attention to the sides of buildings. Look at the sidewalks. Look at the details of the walls in shops.

- What are these surfaces made of?

- What patterns can you find?

- Can you spot geometric shapes?

2 Make rubbings of these patterns when possible. Hold the tracing paper against the surface and rub a crayon or piece of chalk against the paper so the imprint comes through.

- Do certain surfaces use the same patterns?

- Are all sidewalks the same?

- Are all walls the same?

- How are they different?

TRY THIS! Create your own patterns to rub. Using a small amount of clay, you can create patterns on cardboard. Try rolling the clay into long strands or small balls. What other shapes can you make that will create a pattern? Compare your rubbing of the homemade pattern to the rubbings you made of other surfaces. How are they different?

CARTOGRAPHERS ARE MAPMAKERS!

Mapmakers design maps for books, as well as for phone apps and the Internet. They show the world where the streets and buildings—and even our homes—are! You can be a mapmaker, too, with a few supplies and observant eyes.

1 Make a list of things in your neighborhood! What are the parts of your neighborhood? What buildings are in your neighborhood? Are there parks, woods, and highways?

2 Once you have a complete list, assign a number of graph paper blocks to each thing according to how big it is. A school might be a nine while a front yard might be a two.

3 Start drawing streets, roads, walkways, and buildings. Don't forget your own home! Include fields, woods, and streams as much as you can. Think about the number of graphing blocks that you first decided on for each building. You might find you change your number as you draw! How are the streets angled to each other? Where do the houses and other buildings go? How much distance is between each building?

4 When your map is done, find the parallel and perpendicular lines. Go over these in different colors.

5 What shapes can you find? Can you find different polygons and polyhedrons? Color them in different colors. What is the most popular shape in your neighborhood?

TRY THIS! Make another map, but this time, make it of your dream city or town. What buildings do you wish were along the streets and roads? The map can be as fantastical as you want!

MODEL MAKERS

Architects are people who design buildings and structures. Architects need to use models. These small mini-buildings are versions of the big buildings they plan to build. By using a model, architects can show others what their design is and how they plan to build a building. One of the smallest building models was made with just one toothpick! It was a tiny model of the Empire State Building. It holds the Guinness World Record as the "smallest toothpick sculpture." Have you made models before? What are some important things to remember when making a model?

SHAPE DETECTIVE

SUPPLIES

* magnifying glass
* binoculars
* paper
* clipboard
* pencil

Your eyes can be enhanced with magnifying glasses and binoculars. They are extensions of our sight. We can see up close. We can see far away. We can be detectives! It is time to do some investigating.

1 Create a checklist of five different shapes. Draw each one.

2 Observe your neighborhood from the inside and outside of buildings. Tally how many you can find of each shape. Do you see objects with many shapes? Be sure to mark all of them! Write down your list of objects under each shape name.

3 Look closely at small objects, even tiny rocks on the sidewalk. Look to the tippy top of buildings with binoculars to spot special structures. You may see a bell house or a weathervane!

TRY THIS! Double up your list! Be on the hunt for both 2-D and 3-D shapes.

THE NEIGHBORHOOD GROCERY STORE

Talk about shapes! They are in every aisle of the grocery store. Oranges and honeydew melons—spheres! Boxes of pasta are rectangular prisms. Even the shelves are long, long rectangles. The buttons on the cashiers' registers are little cubes. What other shapes can you find? What tools would you use to measure these shapes?

POOL PLANNING

SUPPLIES

* pencil
* graph paper
* ruler
* optional markers and crayons

Take a dip into your own pool, designed and planned by you! Planning this type of project is common. Many city planners, homeowners, building designers, property developers, and construction workers plan such projects.

1 Imagine you want to put a rectangular pool in your community or behind your home. Start a diagram using one or two squares per foot.

2 How long and wide will your pool be? How deep? Depth and height can be the same thing, but one measures down while the other measures up.

3 Calculate length x width x height (L x W x H). That is the volume of how much water will be needed to fill the pool.

4 Now, measure the perimeter of the pool. Add the four sides together to find it.

5 Decorate your diagram with color if you choose!

TRY THIS! Add a hot tub or jacuzzi on the side of the pool. What is the volume? What is the perimeter? Add these smaller pools of water to your diagram. What other bodies of water can you add to your diagram?

PROJECT!

VOLUME SCAVENGER HUNT

Volume is not just found in pools of water. Measurements of length, width, and height or depth can be found all over the neighborhood!

1 Find 3-D objects in your neighborhood that you can measure, such as a mailbox. Make a chart in your math journal with columns for object, length, width, height/depth, and volume.

2 Measure the lengths, the widths, and the heights or depths of the objects you find.

3 Find the volumes of the objects by multiplying length x width x height/depth. If the object is a triangular prism, which is a 3-D shape with a triangle base, you will multiply half of the bottom side times the height.

4 What objects have the largest volume? What objects have the smallest volume? What do you notice about the size of an object and its volume?

TRY THIS! Use a tape measure or yardstick instead of a 12-inch ruler. This will give you many more inches to work with! You can measure larger objects in your neighborhood, such as a chalkboard sign in front of a restaurant. You can calculate the volumes of these objects and discover some larger numbers!

CHAPTER 5

A WIDE WORLD OF GEOMETRY

Nature. The great outdoors! Great enough for . . . math! Geometrical patterns are found in nature more than you might think. Geometry is a part of everything you see, outdoors and beyond, from the flowers to the trees to the solar system.

Remember, patterns are a big part of geometry. Weather follows a pattern. Temperatures follow a pattern. The petals of flowers follow a pattern. The planets in orbit follow a pattern. In nature, there are lots of patterns!

? INVESTIGATE!

Why are there so many examples of the Fibonacci pattern in nature?

fractal: a repeating or mirroring pattern that gets more complex the closer you look at it.

WORDS TO KNOW

Can you picture the patterns you have seen on animals? Think of a snake's skin or a lizard's tail. Think about a raccoon tail or a lemur! What about a zebra's stripes or a giraffe's spots? These are all patterns found in nature.

More patterns can be found in snowflakes, clouds, and even seashells! Let's take a look.

SNOWFLAKES AND FRACTAL PATTERNS

Have you ever looked at snowflake through a magnifying glass? What do you see? Each snowflake has its own unique pattern. The frozen water in snowflakes follows a fractal pattern.

A fractal is formed from a pattern that spirals or mirrors itself. A fractal gets more and more complex and unique the closer you look at it.

jagged fractal: a pattern that does not follow a set pathway.

WORDS TO KNOW

When water crystallizes, it makes patterns that repeat. This is true for frost, too. Have you ever seen frost on a car windshield or on your bedroom window? These patterns are made from repeating images. Each one is its own design. They are unique, like you and your friend, your teacher, and your family. Each one is beautiful in its own way.

Where else can we find such dynamic patterns in nature? Next time there is a thunderstorm, peek out of your window. You might see a lightning bolt in the sky. Lightning is another fractal! The pathway of the lightning bolt is a jagged fractal. It zigs and zags! Each bolt is made up of jagged lines. It does not travel in straight lines.

TRY THIS!

Fractals are very easy to create. Draw a Y shape in your math journal. Then, on every branch of your Y, draw another Y. And then, on every branch of those Ys, draw more Ys. Keep doing this as long as you'd like! This is a fractal. You are repeating a pattern over and over to create a design.

meteorologist: a scientist who studies the weather.

WORDS ⓉⓄ KNOW

Even the thunder that happens along with the lightning bolt has a fractal sound. The sound is caused by the superheating of the air. The time it takes the thunder to reach you ear can depend on distance. The thunder rumbles in fractal patterns.

Using your sight and your hearing, you can experience fractals in nature. What about clouds? Yes! They are fractals, too. Clouds are made up of liquid water droplets.

DID YOU KNOW?

In 1887, a giant snowflake fell in Montana! It was the largest snowflake that was ever recorded—15 inches wide!

When the cloud gets full of water, rain will fall. The clouds form in fractal patterns in the sky. Clouds might look soft and fluffy, but when a meteorologist uses a special camera to zoom in close, they can see the water droplets that make up the cloud and spot the fractal design at work!

WILSON BENTLEY'S SNOWFLAKES

The man who first said, "No two snowflakes are alike," was Wilson Bentley. He was born in the small town of Jericho, Vermont. He was a farmer who loved to take photos of snowflakes. Farmer Bentley paid close attention to the crystals. He was the first person to ever photograph a single snowflake, way back in 1885!

PS Take a look at Wilson Bentley's snowflakes. Can you find the fractal patterns?

KEYWORD PROMPTS

Wilson Bentley's snowflakes 🔍

FIBONACCI AND THE GOLDEN RATIO

Almost 1,000 years ago, Leonardo Fibonacci (c. 1170–1240) figured out a pattern called the Fibonacci sequence! He found a number pattern that goes like this: 1, 1, 2, 3, 5, 8, 13, 21 . . . .

Notice that 1 + 1 = 2. And 2 + 1 = 3. And 3 + 2 = 5. And 5 + 3 = 8. And 8 + 5 = 13. Do you see how the series continues? If this pattern is graphed on graphing paper, it makes a very cool spiral. The Fibonacci sequence is also called the "Golden Ratio."

WHY WAS 13 AFRAID OF 5?

Because 5, 8, 13.

This spiral is found in nature. Notice the numbers of petals on flowers. Take a close look at leaves on a tree. Look at the outside of a pineapple. Peek at the rows of spiraling seeds in the center of a sunflower. Slice a banana and closely look at the center of the banana. Where else can you find a spiral in nature?

Sometimes, the Fibonacci sequence happens in places we can't see with our eyes. Let's think about the honeybee family tree. There are three kinds of honeybees—the queen bee, the worker bees, and the drone bees. The drone bees do not work. But the family tree of the drone bee follows a sequence!

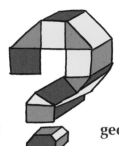

DID YOU KNOW?

Sea creatures called mollusks have shells that are shaped like tubes and coils. More geometry in the sea!

ALWAYS EAT YOUR FIBONACCI!

The Fibonacci sequence appears in vegetables! There is a vegetable called a Romanesco that is much like broccoli. It has many bumps. And on each bump, there is a spiral. There are more spirals that appear on top of those spirals! Artichokes, pineapples, and Brussels sprouts are more foods that display the Fibonacci sequence. Does this mean we can even eat geometry? Delicious!

CREDIT: JON SULLIVAN

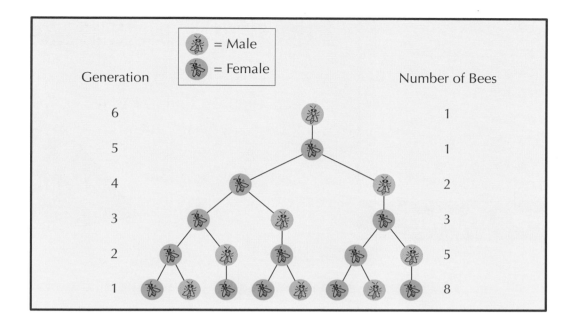

A drone bee is a male bee with one female parent. The drone bee has two grandparents because his mother had two parents. He has three great-grandparents. His grandmother had two parents, but his grandfather only had one. How about great-great-grandparents? Five! And great-great-great-grandparents? Eight! There is the sequence so far: 1, 1, 2, 3, 5, 8. And it goes on!

We can find the Fibonacci sequence in other places, too. The nautilus shell has a special spiral that shows us Fibonacci's sequence at its finest. The top of a conch shell also has this swirl of geometry!

molecule: a group of atoms, which are the smallest particles of matter.

crystal: a solid with its molecules arranged in a repeated pattern.

geode: a hollow piece of stone lined with crystals.

rover: a slow-moving vehicle used to explore planets.

WORDS ᴛᴏ KNOW

TETRAHEDRONS IN NATURE

A tetrahedron is a 3-D shape you learned about in Chapter 2. It is a kind of pyramid with four triangular faces, six straight edges, and four vertices, or corners.

Like the Fibonacci sequence, this shape appears in nature. There are certain molecules that are in the shape of a tetrahedron! Ice crystals take the shape of tetrahedrons, as do the crystal structures in rocks and geodes. The tetrahedron shape is another form of a fractal, because it is made up of many repeating triangles.

DID YOU KNOW? ‑ ‑ ‑ ‑ ‑ ‑

NASA has used robotic rovers to explore the planet Mars. These rovers are often in the shape of a tetrahedron. This allows for a safe landing and better movement.

Geometry is more than just shapes and angles. Geometry is found in our bodies and on our bodies. We can make shapes and angles with our bodies. Geometry is in the classroom, the backyard, the neighborhood, and nature. Always observe the world around you. There is geometry waiting to be discovered . . . and measured!

? CONSIDER AND DISCUSS

It's time to consider and discuss: Why are there so many examples of the Fibonacci pattern in nature?

PROJECT!
FRACTAL FINDER

SUPPLIES

* magnifying glass
* binoculars
* math journal and pencil

Fractals are found in nature, and not just in snowflakes. There are many things in nature that show us fractals at their finest.

Caution: Never look directly at the sun.

1 Use a magnifying glass to look at a snowflake on your jacket. Can you see a fractal pattern? Draw the pattern in your math journal. Is it easier to draw the outside edge of the snowflake or to figure out the pattern and draw the repeating parts?

2 Find a pinecone and look for its fractal patterns. Draw the patterns you discover in your math journal.

3 Use binoculars to peer at the clouds in the sky. In your math journal, draw the patterns you see along the edges of the clouds

4 The next time a storm happens, look at a lightning bolt through binoculars. Watch how jagged it is! Then listen for the fractal rumble of thunder.

5 Ask an adult to cut a pineapple in half for you. Can you find fractal patterns inside? Draw them in your math journal.

TRY THIS! Keep a weather journal. Look outside and fractal hunt every week, or even every day. Notice fractals in weather patterns and how they change depending on the weather. Are you seeing fractals or jagged fractals?

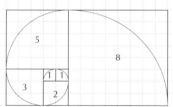

FINDING FIBONACCI

SUPPLIES

* shells with spirals, such as conch or nautilus
* graph paper
* pencil

The Golden Ratio is present in nature, and it can be reproduced easily on graph paper. When constructing the sequence, follow the number pattern carefully. Be sure to turn your paper so you can follow this sacred swirl.

1 Locate shells with spirals, such as conch shells or snail shells.

2 Draw the Fibonacci pattern on graph paper. Follow the pattern: 1, 1, 2, 3, 5, 8, 13, 21 . . . .

3 Compare and contrast your drawing on the graph paper with a conch shell. What are some of the similarities? What is different about the two images?

4 Find other examples of the Golden Ratio in nature and compare them to your diagram. Are some patterns closer to your drawing than others? Why might this be?

TRY THIS! At an aquarium, or even at the beach, you can find many diferent sea creatures. Do you notice the Golden Ratio on any parts of these creatures? Remember the pattern when you look at the number of legs!

PROJECT!

TETRAHEDRON TENT

SUPPLIES

* small sticks
* large leaves
* a cozy spot under the stars
* sunflower seed

Tents are tetrahedrons, or pyramids, we can sleep in! Tents are great for camping. They are structures that keep you warm, dry, and safe. Have you ever set up a tent from a store? Or have you ever made your own? Make a miniature tent!

1 Prop the sticks up in triangular shapes. Lean the sticks together to form a pyramid. The base, or bottom, is the ground.

2 Now design another tent in the shape of a tetrahedron. What are the differences between the two? Which one is taller? Which one is sturdier? Which one will hold more sleepers?

WHY WASN'T THE GEOMETRY TEACHER AT SCHOOL?

She sprained her angle!

3 Place leaves on the outside of the sticks of one of the tents. These are the faces of the tent!

4 Put a little snack in the tent. Maybe a sunflower seed? A small animal might find a bite to eat!

TRY THIS! Make your own tent to sleep in! What materials can you use to make the tetrahedron or pyramid shape that will work best for you? What can you use as your base? How will you get your tent to stay standing when the breeze blows?

PROJECT!
GLOSSARY GAME

Use words from the text and the glossary to create a silly story.

- **noun:** a person, place, or thing
- **plural noun:** more than one person, place, or thing
- **adjective:** a word that describes a noun
- **verb:** an action word
- **adverb:** a word that describes a verb

Kelvin was observing a thunderstorm from his _____. He noticed
(NOUN)

the large _____ coming from the _____ clouds above. The
(PLURAL NOUN)   (ADJECTIVE)

sky was _____ and the storm was getting _____. There were
(ADJECTIVE)   (ADJECTIVE)

large rain _____ that were _____ from the sky. The wind
(PLURAL NOUN)   (VERB WITH –ING)

was roaring and the _____ shook. This make Kelvin feel _____!
(NOUN)   (ADJECTIVE)

But he wanted to _____ anyway.
(VERB)

Suddenly, a loud clap of _____ rang in Kelvin's ears. Then, there
(NOUN)

was a _____ bolt of lightning. Kelvin _____ the curtains. The
(ADJECTIVE)   (ADVERB)

wind _____. He was done _____ out of the window. Instead,
(VERB WITH –ED)   (VERB WITH –ING)

he felt like _____ under his _____! Just when he went to
(VERB WITH –ING)   (NOUN)

his _____, his mother called, "Kelvin, the _____ is over. Come
(NOUN)   (NOUN)

have _____ at the table, please." Kelvin was _____!
(NOUN)   (ADJECTIVE)

A

acute: an angle less than 90 degrees.

angle: the space between two lines that start from the same point, measured in degrees.

architect: a person who designs structures.

area: the surface of an object.

B

BCE: put after a date, BCE stands for Before Common Era and counts years down to zero. CE stands for Common Era and counts years up from zero. This book was published in 2017 CE.

blueprint: a model or detailed plan to follow.

C

chariot: a small cart with two wheels and a platform, pulled by horses.

circa (c.): around that year.

complex: having many parts. The opposite of simple.

congruent: when two shapes are the same as each other.

crop: a plant grown for food and other uses.

crystal: a solid with its molecules arranged in a repeated pattern.

cube: a 3-D shape with six faces, each with four sides, like a square.

cubic feet: a unit of volume that measures length times width times depth (or height), in feet.

culture: a group of people and their beliefs and way of life.

cylinder: a solid figure with straight parallel sides shaped into a circle or an oval, like a can of soup or a paper towel roll.

D

degree: a unit of measurement of angles.

depth: how deep something is, the measurement that gives a shape 3-D qualities.

dilation: the motion of something getting larger or smaller.

dimension: any line of a shape that can be measured.

E

edge: the line where two faces come together.

engineer: someone who uses science, math, and creativity to design and build things.

equidistant: at equal distances.

equilateral: a type of triangle with three equal sides.

equivalent: when the measurements of different shapes are the same.

F

face: the flat side of a 3-D shape.

Fibonacci sequence: a series of numbers where each number is the sum of the two preceding numbers: 1, 1, 2, 3, 5, 8, 13 . . . .

fractal: a repeating or mirroring pattern that gets more complex the closer you look at it.

G

geode: a hollow piece of stone lined with crystals.

geometry: the math related to shapes, surfaces, points, lines, and solids.

glacier: a slowly moving mass of ice and snow.

gravity: a force that pulls objects toward each other, and all objects to the earth.

grid: a network of evenly spaced horizontal and perpendicular lines.

H

harmony: a pleasing blend of sounds.

height: the measure of how tall an object is.

hemisphere: half of a sphere.

horizontal: straight across from side to side.

hypotenuse: the side of a right triangle that is opposite the right angle. It is always the longest side of a right triangle.

I

intersect: lines that cross over or meet.

isosceles: a type of triangle with two equal sides and one that is not equal.

J

jagged fractal: a pattern that does not follow a set pathway.

L

layout: the way the parts of something are arranged.

length: the measure of something from one end to the other, or how long something is.

line of symmetry: the imaginary line where you can fold a shape or picture and each half matches exactly.

line segment: two connected points that create a line.

lines: many points in a row that make one length.

M

mathematics: the study of ideas related to numbers. Mathematicians study mathematics.

Mesopotamia: an area of ancient civilization between the Tigris and Euphrates Rivers in what is now called Iraq, Kuwait, and Syria.

meteorologist: a scientist who studies the weather.

metric: the units of measurement based on the number 10. The metric system includes centimeters and meters, grams and kilograms.

molecule: a group of atoms, which are the smallest particles of matter.

N

numerical value: a term to show numbers and their worth.

O

obtuse: an angle more than 90 degrees.

origami: the ancient art of paper-folding.

P

parallel: lines that are side by side, with space between them.

parallelogram: a four-sided shape with opposite parallel sides.

pattern: a series of repetitive connections and designs.

pentagon: a shape with five sides.

perimeter: the boundary of a shape.

perpendicular: a line at an angle of 90 degrees to another line or surface. The two lines form a corner, called a right angle.

point: a spot in space or on a line.

polygon: a shape with three or more straight sides and angles.

polyhedron: a 3-D shape.

prism: a solid shape whose two end faces are similar, equal, and parallel and whose sides are parallelograms.

pyramid: a shape with a square base and triangles for sides that meet at a point.

Q

quadrilateral: any shape with four sides.

R

rectangle: a shape with four sides and four right angles. The sides across from each other are equal.

reflection: a mirror image.

rhombus: a shape with four equal sides that has opposite equal acute and obtuse angles and opposite equal parallel sides.

rhythm: a pattern of beats.

right angle: an angle that measures exactly 90 degrees, as at the corner of a square or rectangle.

right triangle: a triangle with a right angle.

rotate: to turn like a wheel around a fixed point.

rover: a slow-moving vehicle used to explore planets.

S

scale: a tool used to weigh objects.

scalene: a type of triangle with three sides that do not equal one another.

slope: the incline of a line.

solar calendar: a yearly calendar based on how long it takes the earth to move around the sun.

sphere: a round shape that looks like a ball.

square: a shape with four equal sides and four right angles.

square inch: a unit of area that measures length times width, in inches.

standard measurement: the units of measurement used in the United States, such as inches and feet, ounces and pounds.

symmetry: when a shape is the same when it is flipped, turned, or moved.

T

tally: to count the number of something.

tetrahedron: a 3-D shape with four faces, each with three sides, like a triangle.

three-dimensional (3-D): something that appears solid and can be measured in three directions.

trapezoid: a quadrilateral with a pair of parallel sides.

triangle: a shape with three sides.

two-dimensional (2-D): something that appears flat and can only be measured in two directions.

V

vertical: up and down.

vertices: the corners where the lines of a polygon meet.

volume: the amount of space inside a shape.

W

wavelength: the distance between two waves.

weight: the measure of the force of gravity on an object.

width: the measure of something from one end to the other, or how wide something is.

BOOKS

What's Your Angle, Pythagoras?
Julie Ellis (Charlesbridge, 2004).

Sir Cumference and the Dragon of Pi
Cindy Neuschwander (Charlesbridge, 1999).

The Greedy Triangle
Marilyn Burns (Scholastic, 2008).

Perimeter, Area, and Volume: A Monster Book of Dimensions
David A. Adler (Holiday House, 2013).

If You Were a Quadrilateral
Molly Blaisdell (Picture Window Books, 2009).

Grandfather Tang's Story
Ann Tompert (Random House, 1997).

Building a Playground
Joshua Rae Martin (Shell Education, 2010).

Terrific Triangles
Lee Anne Snozek (Dover Publications, 2010).

Captain Invincible and the Space Shapes
Stuart J. Murphy (Harper Collins, 2001).

WEBSITES

DK Find Out
dkfindout.com/us/math/geometry

NeoK12
neok12.com/geometry.htm

Flocabulary
flocabulary.com/unit/weve-got-some-shapes

Ducksters
ducksters.com/kidsmath/circle.php

Math Playground
mathplayground.com/index_geometry.html

PBS Kids
pbskids.org/games/shapes

QR CODE GLOSSARY

page 7: youtube.com/watch?v=lYhAAMDQl-Q

page 16: time.com/2848303/heres-what-faces-would-look-like-if-they-were-perfectly-symmetrical

page 37: tate.org.uk/art/art-terms/c/cubism

page 44: exploratorium.edu/ronh/weight

page 51: allaboutbirds.org/guide/search

page 60: graphicdesignnyc.net/2012/06/street-art-video-how-to-do-3d-sidewalk-chalk-paintings

page 72: commons.wikimedia.org/wiki/File:SnowflakesWilsonBentley.jpg

ESSENTIAL QUESTIONS

Introduction: How many different shapes can you
make with your hands and fingers?

Chapter 1: What shapes and angles can you find on your body?

Chapter 2: Are there more polygons or polyhedrons in your classroom?

Chapter 3: What might your house look like if the builder hadn't measured
anything? Why is it important to measure the sizes of things?

Chapter 4: Why is it important to know the area,
perimeter, or volume of a space or object?

Chapter 5: Why are there so many examples of the Fibonacci pattern in nature?

METRIC CONVERSIONS

Use this chart to find the metric
equivalents to the English
measurements in this book. If you
need to know a half measurement,
divide by two. If you need to know
twice the measurement, multiply
by two. How do you find a quarter
measurement? How do you find
three times the measurement?

English	Metric
1 inch	2.5 centimeters
1 foot	30.5 centimeters
1 yard	0.9 meter
1 mile	1.6 kilometers
1 pound	0.5 kilogram
1 teaspoon	5 milliliters
1 tablespoon	15 milliliters
1 cup	237 milliliters